# The Bluffer's®
## Guide to
# Banking

Robert Cooper
Simon Whaley

Oval Books

Published by Oval Books
5 St John's Buildings
Canterbury Crescent
London SW9 7QH
United Kingdom

Telephone: +44 (0)20 7733 8585
Fax: +44 (0)20 7733 8544
E-mail: info@ovalbooks.com
Web site: www.ovalbooks.com

Series Editor – Anne Tauté

Cover designer – Vicki Towers
Cover image – © 2008 Jupiterimages (UK) Ltd.
Printer – J. H. Haynes & Co Ltd., Sparkford
Producer – Oval Projects Ltd.

The Bluffer's® Guides series is based
on an original idea by Peter Wolfe.

The Bluffer's Guide®, The Bluffer's Guides®,
Bluffer's®, and Bluff Your Way® are
Registered Trademarks.

ISBN: 978-1-903096-52-9

# CONTENTS

# INTRODUCTION

Banks. We love them when they agree to lend us money, and hate them when they have the audacity to ask for it back, especially when they demand a lot more to be returned than they handed out in the first place.

**❝ Banks. We love them when they agree to lend us money, and hate them when they have the audacity to ask for it back. ❞**

Banks deal with two types of customers – those that have money, and those that don't. For those who have money (we'll call them savers) they will look after it, keep it safe – if they can – and allow them to withdraw it whenever they like. Usually. The bank will also give those savers some money for allowing them to look after it for them. This money is called interest. This is because the returns on use of the money make it interesting.

For customers who don't have any money (let's call them borrowers), the banks will lend them some, using the money that the savers have left in their safekeeping. The banks then charge those borrowers without money even more money for the privilege of borrowing. This is also called interest and, cunningly, is at a higher rate than is given to the savers whose money they are using. This makes it even more interesting.

If you've been paying attention, you will realise

that bankers act as intermediaries – the middlemen of money – and it is the difference between rates that allow them to make a profit. Usually, a large profit. Often, a very large profit.

There is, of course, more than one way to skin a cat (or fleece a customer) and it's in any bank's interest to know them all. The banking industry takes great pains to portray itself as a flexible one, bending over backwards to offer specially tailored 'products' to those who need them. Or those who might be persuaded they need them once they know that they exist. The first skill you need, therefore, is to bluff your way to obtaining the ones that are useful to you, and avoid those that aren't.

> **66 There is, of course, more than one way to skin a cat (or fleece a customer) and it's in any bank's interest to know them all. 99**

It is obviously to your advantage, therefore, to know something about the background to this giant industry that in the UK alone juggles over one trillion pounds' worth of personal debt, some of which is probably yours.

This guide to banking will arm you with sufficient information to make the bankers take you seriously as a customer. It should enrich you mentally and could make you richer financially. You may even change your position in the money chain and become someone from whom the banks borrow, rather than someone who borrows from the banks.

# MONEY AND BANKING

It's a well-known maxim that money makes the world go around, and banking is the greasing agent that smoothes this process. If the banks don't have money, the world doesn't so much spin round, as scrunch. A wise bluffer will be keen to appreciate how this came about. It would also be prudent for some banks to learn the basics once more too.

## A brief history

The origins of banking date way back in time to a period that we shall refer to as BC – 'Before Cash'. Mesopotamia, home to the most advanced civilisation on the planet at the time (around 3000 in the real BC era) is where it all started – or so most historians believe. It was so civilised, that the only safe

> 66 It's a well-known maxim that money makes the world go around – and banking is the greasing agent that smoothes this process. 99

place to store anything of value was in the royal palaces, or temples of worship.

## Coins and cash

It wasn't until much later, around 700 BC that the first metal coins appeared in China, and simultaneously in Lydia (present-day Turkey). The Greeks and Romans followed not far behind and some of their coins still exist today, and are highly valued by collectors, although not by shopkeepers. This information won't do you much good when asking your bank manager for a loan, but knowing it may give you an inner glow of superiority.

Coins may have been invented to resolve embarrassing bartering difficulties. If a peasant farmer owned three chickens but needed a pig, and the going rate for a pig was two and a half chickens, then he was in trouble. Of course, early bluffers would have excelled in this situation, pointing out that their chickens were exceptional at laying high-quality eggs, and that two such hens were easily worth three on the open market. They may even have pointed out that two birds in the hand were worth three in the bush. Coinage made the world an easier place to live, but took all the fun out of small transactions for such bartering connoisseurs.

> **If a peasant farmer owned three chickens but needed a pig, and the going rate for a pig was two and a half chickens, then he was in trouble.**

The concept of borrowing money, and paying interest for doing so, can be laid at the door of the Roman Empire. As well as taking deposits of precious commodities and issuing receipts, they hit upon the real money-making area of banking – loans. After conquering Britain, they introduced their new, highly sophisticated banking system to their new colony –

rather like any other organisation, which imposes its own terms and conditions following a takeover.

## Banknotes

In Britain, many people stored their money and valuables in the churches and abbeys, until Henry VIII began the reformation of the church and the dissolution of the monasteries (1536). With religious buildings being ransacked and destroyed, they were no longer the safe havens that they used to be. Those who needed somewhere safe to store their valuables now turned to a new breed of gentlemen – goldsmiths.

> 66 Because of the value of their raw materials, goldsmiths took security very seriously indeed, ensuring that their premises were heavily protected. 99

Because of the value of their raw materials, goldsmiths took security very seriously indeed, ensuring that their premises were heavily protected from unwanted attack. This made them the safest places (as safe as the 16th century permitted – the bank robber's favourite accessory, the stocking, wasn't invented until the 1930s) to keep valuables and cash, and laid the foundations for the modern banking system. One customer would give his goldsmith written instructions, in lieu of payment, to pay money to another of the goldsmith's customers. Thus the very first cheques were born.

Receipts issued by the goldsmith as evidence of a deposit were often used to demonstrate to third parties the customer's ability to pay – and thus bank-notes were born. Think of them as an early form of I.O.U. – their essence reflected in the phrase 'I promise to pay the bearer...'

## The major institutions

In order to feel confident at bluffing in banking, the aspiring bluffer needs to know a little bit about the background of the major institutions. The following may help to clear a path through this particular financial forest.

### The Bank of England

Welcome to the bank with no branches. The Bank of England, known as the Old Lady of Threadneedle Street (after its site in the City of London) was set up in 1694, when several London merchants proposed the creation of a central bank which could lend money to the government during times of war, and for building the country's economy during peacetime, and is not a typical bank. It doesn't offer credit cards, or Instant Access

**66 The Bank of England was set up with just one customer in mind – the government. It now also holds accounts for other banks, which makes it the bankers' bank. 99**

6

Savings accounts or online banking. It was set up with just one customer in mind – the government. It now also holds accounts for other banks, which makes it the bankers' bank and (apart from the tax-payer) lender of last resort.

Since 1997, the Bank of England's Monetary Policy Committee has been in charge of interest rates. These rates have been one popular method of controlling the economy. Bluffers know that such methods are not in every-body's interest. Whether they be savers or shoppers, whichever way the rates move there are always winners and losers.

**❝In Scotland and Northern Ireland individual banks still have the ability to issue their own notes.❞**

The Bank of England is the only financial institution in England and Wales permitted to issue notes and coins. In Scotland and Northern Ireland, individual banks still have the ability to issue their own notes, which means that if you want to trick your children into thinking that they're going abroad for a summer holiday, head north of Gretna Green (or south if travelling from the other direction). Not only is the money different, but the dialects vary too.

However, for every note these banks print, they must have a deposit of equal value held at the Bank of England.

Banknotes from Northern Ireland are generally

not accepted in England, but Scottish notes usually are. Rather magnanimously, the Scots and the Irish will accept English notes.

The worst job at the Bank of England must be that of the Chief Cashier. It's his (or her – for there has been a female Chief Cashier) signature that appears on every new note printed. More than 700 million notes are issued every year – that's 700 million signatures and a lot of ink.

### The big four

This is the collective term for the four biggest high street banks in England and Wales, which have about 7,000 branches between them. They are listed in alphabetical order, not in order of profitability – the financial world is far too uncertain.

**Barclays:** Operates in more than 30 countries and was the first bank in the UK to offer credit cards through its Barclaycard subsidiary. The bank is easily recognised by its eagle logo. Remember that the eagle is a bird of prey, with some of the fiercest feet and talons in the animal kingdom, perfect for ripping its quarry to shreds, once it has a tight grip on them.

> 66 Barclays bank is easily recognised by its eagle logo. Remember that the eagle is a bird of prey. 99

**HSBC** (Hong Kong Shanghai Banking Corporation, known in the trade as Honkers and Shaggers): Opened its first European office in London in 1865. In 1992, HSBC bought Midland Bank – in which it already had a share – and the latter's logo of a yellow griffin was replaced by a strange little red and white lozenge. It may occur to bluffers that lozenges are usually swallowed by suckers.

> **The griffin was replaced by a strange little red and white lozenge. It may occur to a shrewd bluffer that lozenges are usually swallowed by suckers.**

**Lloyds TSB:** Lloyds first opened its doors in Birmingham in 1765. The bank expanded rapidly in the 20th century, with mergers and take-overs across Europe, South America and the southern hemisphere In 1995, it acquired the Cheltenham & Gloucester and then merged with the TSB Group to form Lloyds TSB. The bank is recognised by its black horse logo, which in 2008 went from being not so much a charger as almost due for the knacker's yard. It then fancied itself as a white knight – see Bank of Scotland.

**The National Westminster Bank (NatWest** to its friends): Created in 1968, when the National Provincial Bank linked up with the Westminster Bank. The Royal Bank of Scotland Group pulled off the largest ever take-over in the history of British banking (at the time) by acquiring Natwest in 2000. It continues to trade under its own name and has so far maintained its logo of three arrowheads, although such bellicose posturing failed to stop an attack from north of the border.

## In Scotland

**Bank of Scotland (BOS):** Established by an Act of Parliament of Scotland in 1695, it should not be confused with Royal Bank of Scotland. Traditionally, there has always been rivalry between England and Scotland. The fact that the Bank of Scotland was founded by an Englishman, just 12 months after a Scotsman founded the Bank of England, demonstrates that such rivalry wasn't confined to the battlefields. Modern day skirmishes only occur in the bedroom after this Scottish Bank married the very English Halifax to form **HBOS** (note how the acronym would not have worked the other way round).

> **The Scots are known for their canniness with money, and it was the Royal Bank of Scotland that invented the overdraft facility.**

During the credit crunch, Lloyds TSB jumped out of the closet, got down on one knee and proposed marriage. This forced the government to agree to rewrite legislation to allow bigamy – which was big of them. It was clearly seen as a match made in heaven, otherwise the government wouldn't have offered the indebted ménage umpteen billion to put their nuptials on solid foundations.

**Clydesdale Bank:** Created in 1838 in Glasgow it has focused on serving the rural communities and wide-open spaces of West Scotland and Aberdeenshire. This may explain why it is now owned by the National Australian Bank Group, which also knows a lot about wide-open spaces.

**Lloyds TSB Scotland:** The TSB (Trustees Savings Bank) was begun in the Scottish Borders in 1810 by the Reverend Henry Duncan who wanted to help his poorest parishioners to save money during the good years to help tide them over during the bad. This method of banking proved popular and only eight years later there were 465 individual savings banks across the UK. It became a wholly owned subsidiary of the Lloyds TSB Group.

**Royal Bank of Scotland:** The **RBS** opened for business in Edinburgh in 1727 and started issuing its own banknotes immediately. The Scots are known for their canniness with money, and it was this bank that invented the overdraft facility just 12 months later.

### In Northern Ireland

**Bank of Ireland:** The Bank of Ireland (**BOI**), in existence since the 1780s, has its head office in the republic's capital, Dublin, yet has a large network of branches across Northern Ireland. Most banks have a

Board of Directors but BOI, rather grandly, has a 'Court' and at the Court's Annual General Meeting, the CEO has to stand trial to account for his year's stewardship. He has rarely been found guilty.

**First Trust Bank:** Created by the Irish Banking organisation, Allied Irish Banks. Some may think that the presence of the words 'First' and 'Trust' in a bank's title is trying a little too hard to boost customer confidence.

**Northern Bank:** Started life as the Northern Banking Partnership in Belfast and grew into the largest retail bank in Northern Ireland. In 2004 it was acquired by the Danish Banking Group, Danske. Nineteen days later, the biggest bank robbery ever to have taken place occurred at the bank's HQ in Belfast when £26.5 million walked out the back door. An extreme reaction to a perceived Viking invasion perhaps, but the loss was so enormous the bank had to replace all its notes with a new design.

> **Some may think that the presence of the words 'First' and 'Trust' in a bank's title is trying a little too hard.**

**Ulster Bank:** Established in 1836 it ultimately amalgamated with the London County & Westminster Bank to improve its financial stability. Now a part of the Royal Bank of Scotland Group.

## What banks do with their millions

When customers hear about the banks' bumper billion pound profits, they tend to see red... at the size of their bank charges. But bluffers should remind infuriated friends that it is vital for banks to have profits, however unpalatable it seems. Explain that what banks do with their profits (aside from extravagant rewards to their executives (a.k.a. 'masters of the universe') is:

1. **Reward their shareholders.** The banks are companies and they have shareholders, both individual and corporate, who have a stake in the company. In stable times, buying shares in profit-generating banks is quite a sharp move for those who are not of a nervous disposition. If banks are going to make a profit out of you, you may as well make a profit out of them.

> **"If banks are going to make a profit out of you, you may as well make a profit out of them."**

If a credit, liquidity or banking crisis causes share prices to plummet, such action is open to debate. Nevertheless, bluffers with an eye to the main chance will of course buy tons of bank shares at rock bottom prices comfortable in the knowledge that all banks can't be allowed to fail. And as long as market capitalism survives, the shares of the banks that survive will inevitably rise again thus allowing the bluffer to bask in a 'told you so' glow.

2. **Meet 'capital adequacy ratios'**. The regulatory authorities (the FSA and the Bank of England) require that banks ensure they have sufficient working capital available to keep trading, despite bad debts which might arise. Each year a sum of money gets set aside for this from the profits. As these sums were deemed insufficient in the credit crisis, suggest this be more aptly called 'capital inadequacy ratios'.

3. **Expand their business** and invest in other related activities, such as the acquisition of insurance companies (e.g., the ownership of Direct Line Insurance and Churchill by the Royal Bank of Scotland). Diversification serves to safeguard banks in unpredictable circumstances. Global events notwithstanding, the one thing they can count on is a link in the public mind between banks and safety (deposit boxes etc.), so they have hit upon the bright idea of offering peace of mind re the unpredictable, in the form of data back-ups for customers' PCs. After all, they are experts in crashes and securities.

4. **Weather other storms** in the markets – unless on the scale of the tsunami precipitated by the failure of the sub-prime market, when some were washed away while others had to be bailed out. A bluffer keen to remain ahead of the wave, would be wise to digest the following:

14

**Sub-prime lending**

Before the banking world was turned upside down, i.e., before the Credit Crunch (BCC), a crappy asset racket came a-cropper in America. It was otherwise known as the US sub-prime mortgage market.

"The reason the UK banks became involved," you will say – with all the confidence of one-who-knows – "is that in normal market conditions the sub-prime mortgage market gave banks a good return, one that was considerably higher than the return on their own customers' deposits which were used to fund it. So the UK banks participated by buying parcels of debt from the US banks, which left the US banks with cash to enable them to make further loans to the US housing market." The bluffer will note that 'sub' means below and is therefore Not A Good Thing. In a nutshell, sub-prime lending means selling mortgages to people who cannot afford them, and charging them more than those who can.

> **❝In a nutshell, sub-prime lending means selling mortgages to people who cannot afford them, and charging them more than those who can.❞**

It doesn't take a bluffer to twig that this was doomed even without the schemes devised by financial whizz-kids that allowed banks and other mortgage lenders to 'package up' lots of individual sub-prime mortgages and sell them on to other financial institutions around the world, by way of 'securitisation'. Other terms such as Collateralised Debt Obligations (CDOs) and Structured Investment Vehicles (SIVs) are also useful for the bluffer to bandy about but under no circumstances be drawn into an attempt to explain them. Even the so-called experts struggle with these.

When sub-prime customers began to default on their loans, banks realised that they were going to lose money. (Although unlike the mortgagees they weren't going to lose their homes.) But if there's one thing bankers don't like, it's losing money. It's not what they're there for.

**❝ If there's one thing bankers don't like, it's losing money. It's not what they're there for. ❞**

Bluffers who have been paying attention thus far will realise that the potential for default was now not just between customers and banks but between banks and banks. Money markets went into crisis mode, with billions of dollars written off the bottom line, and financial institutions becoming reluctant to lend money to each other because of no certainty of repayment. Thus, a liquidity crisis ensued, with banks unable to finance normal banking activities and the 'cash is king' theory, unpopular for some time, returned as the mantra of the worldly wise.

If conversations turn to the subject of sub-prime lending, as they are wont to do, you could simply observe that you agree with Shakespeare's ditty:

'Neither a borrower nor a lender be; For loan oft loses both itself and friend'.

## Northern Rock and others

Alas, this was not a policy followed by Northern Rock. They had borrowed short (i.e. taken short term deposits from the banks in the inter bank market) and had lent long (i.e., on mortgage loans which would not be paid for a long time – if ever). Thus the Bank of England was forced to step in to enable Northern Rock to meet their short term obligations. This was officially described as a 'liquidity support facility', and no doubt a lot of liquid support was needed at the time.

> **" This was officially described as a 'liquidity support facility', and no doubt a lot of liquid support was needed at the time. "**

## Global bank nationalisations

Bluffers who sat on the sidelines, listening to the sound of credit crunching, will know that Northern Rock turned out to be a mere pebble in the beach of possible bankruptcies when compared to others around the world. In the UK, banks like HBOS, Lloyds TSB and the Royal Bank of Scotland were asking the government to splash the cash. By effectively buying shares in the banks, the government

was undertaking the biggest nationalisation pro-
gramme since the Second World War. Bluffers
should tell friends not to worry about this. As long
as they continue to pay bank charges, the banks will
continue to make a profit, which means that they
can then pay the government dividends, so the government doesn't have to raise taxes. This will leave
more money in one's pockets (because of not paying
even higher taxes) ... or in their bank account ... or
not, if one is overdrawn and paying bank charges.
Well, you get the drift, if not the money back.

To the non-bluffer this plan may seem thoroughly
confusing, which is why governments around the
world decided that the British plan was a Good Plan
and followed suit, buying up their
own banks. Iceland nationalised all
three of its own.

> **The phrase Mum's gone to Iceland took on a whole new meaning (to get her money back).**

Nationalisation wasn't the only
solution though. Bradford &
Bingley staff suddenly woke up
one morning and had to quickly learn Spanish when
they were taken over by the Santander group. In
America, famous names like Lehman Brothers (the
fourth largest US investment bank) filed for bank-
ruptcy protection, allowing the sharp talons of the
Barclay's eagle to swoop in and cherry pick the profitable meat whilst leaving the toxic mortgage debts
on the carcass.

Merrill Lynch was taken over by the Bank of America, while Morgan Stanley was propped up by a Japanese Bank. When Icelandic banks suddenly prevented UK savers from withdrawing their money, the UK government retaliated by freezing Icelandic assets held in the UK. The phrase, "Mum's gone to Iceland," took on a whole new meaning (to get her money back), whilst Anglo-Icelandic relations became as frosty as they were in the 1950s and 1970s during the Cod Wars.

## DEALING WITH BANKS

Banks don't deal just with an amorphous being called a customer, they deal with customers who are at 'personal stages' in their lives, each one of which demands what they perceive as the right 'products' for you at your time of life. So, if you know your life stage, you should know what to expect from your bank. And get used to the word 'product' – they use it a lot.

### Customer life stages – personal

**0 to 7 years:** This is the best life stage to be in. The under-sevens can't borrow money, but then they don't have to buy anything. Their account will be in the name of a (supposedly) responsible adult and come with a faux-naïve name, free magazine and a 'fun' money box. When the infant account holder is older and the cash point machine has swallowed his or her card they may wish they had kept the tardis-shaped money box because then they would have an emergency supply of cash.

**The difficult teenage years:** With age comes responsibility – and, it is to be hoped, height. When young people can physically reach the cash point machine, their accounts may be changed to a kind that has a card so they can obtain money.

> **❝In an attempt to prepare the teenager for adult life, the cash point card may be upgraded to a debit card with limited functionality.❞**

In an attempt to prepare the teenager for adult life, the cash point card may be upgraded to a debit card with limited functionality. That means they can use it in shops to make purchases, but rather unfairly, they have to have money in their account. This sometimes comes as an unwelcome surprise.

Until they reach the age of 18, young people are not liable for any debts they accrue, which is why many financial institutions won't lend money to a minor. Someone, usually a parent, must act as a guarantor and make the payments if their offspring fail to do so. As many teenagers soon realise, it is better to cut out the bank from this process and go straight to the parents.

**Student life:** Not only can students have a proper current account, but they are entitled to one with a debit card, an overdraft facility that increases annually while they are at university, and a credit card. The banking industry sees students as a long-term investment, which is why they throw all this money (otherwise known as debt) at them. If they take it all up, and it's usually too tempting to resist, they'll be paying the banks back for years. (It's an embryonic form of the sub-prime syndrome.)

This could be regarded as the first really long-term relationship of adult life. Assuming the ex-student survives the traditional three score years and ten, banks estimate that he or she is likely to earn substantially more money

> **"The banking industry sees students as a long-term investment. It's an embryonic form of the sub-prime syndrome."**

than someone who hasn't been to university. However, this will only be enough to pay off student loans, graduate loans, mortgages, car loans, pension plan instalments and any other financial service your ever faithful banker will be only too pleased to provide. Banks will therefore become the indebted account holder's best friend. Or, at least, the one that never goes away.

Some banks will even fall back into old habits and offer you free gifts (usually not cutely-shaped money boxes, however). It is advisable to take as many free gifts as possible. Banking psychology holds that a customer who accepts a gift feels obliged to remain with that particular bank. Self-respecting bluffers should feel free to be promiscuous at this stage of life and move rapidly to the next bank that provides a new free gift. Often.

**Early married life:** The bank will be keen to help the newly married set up home with one of its mortgages, and life assurance to pay off the mortgage when one partner dies. Dire warnings about a surviving partner being left in penury ensure that life assurance policies are taken out. Any potential children must have the best: the bank will be delighted to help young marrieds start saving for school fees now. And helping set up a pension fund so that these children are not burdened later in life with aged, impoverished parents.

> **66** Banks are more than willing to continue serving their customers in death, particularly as this is the area of work in which they receive fewest complaints from their customers. **99**

**Middle age:** It comes to us all, so when the mid-life crisis looms, the bank will be there to help. Need a

22

loan for that Harley Davidson? Certainly sir. And banks know that no-one likes to think about it, but it really is time that sir or madam made a will.

**Pre-retirement:** Children may have flown the nest, but there are always the grandchildren to think about, and a savings account for when they reach 18 will certainly be appreciated (by the bank as well as the grandchildren). And perhaps sir should consider selling the Harley Davidson to top up his pension.

**Retirement:** Banks will advise that retired people review their wills to ensure they are up to date. And if customers need guidance in reducing inheritance tax liability, the bank can help. By charging a fee for this service, the bank automatically reduces the amount of money available to the taxman.

**Death:** Not technically a 'life stage', but banks are more than willing to continue serving their customers in death as executors of the deceased's will, particularly as this is the area of work in which they receive fewest complaints from their customers.

Banks expect everybody to act their age, and bluffers should act the youngest age that they're capable of. It's where all the interesting perks and freebies are to be found.

## Customer life stages – business

Banks treat new businesses rather as they treat students. They extend tempting offers, such as free banking for fixed periods, in the hope that the business will stay with them, flourish and then earn them lots of money in the big wide corporate world. They also throw in a dedicated business manager who is at the end of a phone with free advice. Students do not receive this perk.

**The start-up:** Start-ups tend to be sole traders and partnerships rather than limited companies, so the bank is still dealing with individuals rather than a business organisation. This is a bluffer's paradise. The aim of the game here is to persuade a business banker that a start-up loan of £20,000 is a good investment. Banks hate risk. If they give their money to someone, not only do they want it back, but also they want it back with interest. Lots, if possible.

> **The business start-up bluffer has to prove that he or she doesn't actually need the loan in the first place, in order to get it.**

So the business start-up bluffer has to prove that he or she doesn't actually need the loan in the first place, in order to get it. Be positive at all times and be sure to use the banker's favourite assessment tool, the business plan. This tends to be a document replete with unsubstantiated assumptions and guesswork, so is an exercise any wily bluffer should relish. In terms of creative writing the accomplished business planner can put novelists in the shade.

The plan should be packed full of growth projections, future sales and income figures, and if possible, the future balance of the business current account. Projections should form the main financial part of the business plan and naturally will be the area of most interest to the banker. No self-respecting business banker would dare claim that they didn't understand your document, so make your projections as complicated as you can and be sure to include lots of graphs and coloured pictures.

> **" Some of the business will be conducted in a posh restaurant over lunch. If the bank is hopeful of selling more services, lunch may even be on them. "**

**Corporate clients:** The world of corporate banking is different from personal and small business banking. For a start, some of the business will be conducted in a posh restaurant over lunch. If the bank is hopeful of selling more services, lunch may even be on them. This is because corporate banking is a business-to-business relationship. Both parties appreciate that they are operating to make profits for their shareholders. In the business-to-business world, charges, fees and commissions are expected and respected.

A corporate business customer expects to be charged by another business, including its bankers. Of course, it doesn't expect to be ripped off, so the bank that offers the best deal for its services is the winner. This is where economies of scale work best for a bank. It doesn't cost any more for a bank to operate a corporate bank account with £200 million in it, than it does for one with £15 million in it. The more money held on deposit, though, the more money the bank has to play with overnight on the money markets. And playing with other people's money is what banks like best.

> **The more money held on deposit, the more money the bank has to play with. And playing with other people's money is what banks like best.**

The corporate bluffer's best bargaining tool is to mention that the bank's main competitor has extended a lunch invitation for the following day. If it is possible to convey, in a subtle manner, that it will be at the rival bank's expense, so much the better. The loss of an overnight profit-generating source of funds will make any bank re-consider your overdraft rate.

## Banker/customer relationship

The relationship between banker and customer is similar to that of a marriage. It's a love/hate thing. Using Transaction Analysis (see glossary) as a guide, the relationship can be broken down into three categories. These three categories form the heart of the banking drama and can be utilised by the bluffer to enhance credibility and status.

## 1 Banker as parent, customer as child:

Banker: 'How can I help you?'

Customer: 'I need a loan/mortgage, etc.'

Banker: 'Mmm, you need to borrow some money, do you? Shouldn't you have planned for this eventuality some time ago and started saving to meet the requirement?' (Note the banker terminology, 'eventuality' and 'requirement' which makes the customer feel inadequate and serves to propagate the myth that banking is far more complex than it really is.)

## 2 Banker as adult, customer as adult:

Banker: 'How can I help you?'

Customer: 'I'm thinking of purchasing a house/ investing in property.'

Banker: 'Ah, very wise. So what are you thinking of buying...' (The competent bluffer will answer only direct questions as appropriate and let the banker feel he is trying to get your business rather than you seeking his help. The conversation then becomes one of equals, albeit that some are more equal than others.)

### 3 Banker as child, customer as parent:

Banker: 'How can I help you?'

Customer: 'I'm purchasing a house/investing in property and I'm investigating which bank will deliver the best product.'

Banker (adopting an unctuous tone): 'I can assure you that you won't beat the Sycophantic Bank plc for value and service...'

It goes without saying that you should take the initiative to ensure that the third scenario prevails. Using their terms demonstrates that you know exactly what you need from the banker, without actually articulating it. And it will make the banker/child behave if he is trying to please the bluffer/parent. A most welcome development.

If providing advice to others, however, bluffers should advise the adoption of the scenario 2 approach when dealing with a bank. It wouldn't do to give away all one's insider knowledge.

**❝Using their terms demonstrates that you know exactly what you need from the banker, without actually articulating it.❞**

The biggest bluffers in banking are, of course, students, who should look on dealing with banks as part of their education. After all, the less one has, the more one has to gain, and hence, the greater the need for hornswoggling.

Students are likely to be interrogated (or interviewed as it is known in the banking world) before any money changes hands. When attempting to obtain an overdraft, it is imperative that the supplicant holds his or her nerve. As the interview draws to a close, it is necessary to ask the vital question of the likelihood of the facility being granted. Do not blink. Instead, maintain full eye contact and an air of utmost solemnity until you are out of the door. Never ask in a pleading fashion: the banker will turn tail at the first hint of desperation.

> **66 When attempting to obtain an overdraft, it is imperative that the supplicant holds his or her nerve. 99**

Indeed, the best way to ascertain whether you are likely to get the money is to ask: 'If I am granted the facility, how soon can I access the funds?' This works on three levels:

1 Firstly, using the banking terminology 'granted the facility' and 'access the funds', leads the banker to assume that the student bluffer, although youthful, understands the business of banking and is used to such scenarios. This offers comfort to the banker.

2 Secondly, leading with the phrase 'If I am granted...' infers a suitable lack of presumption about the outcome of the application. This is an absolute must in getting the banker on side.

3 Finally, asking 'when' (rather than 'if') the funds will be available, leads the banker down the path of visualising actually handing over the money. As most people, even bankers, would rather say yes than no, this helps him or her come to the desired decision. Time for a little quiet self-congratulation – cash in hand and a successful bluff chalked up. Your university years have not been wasted.

> **Asking 'when' (rather than 'if') the funds will be available, leads the banker down the path of visualising actually handing over the money.**

# THE BANKERS

## Cashiers

Once the most respected of jobs within the banking industry, achieved only after decades of banking experience and usually about five years before retirement, the post of cashier is now one of the first rungs on the banking career ladder. Almost anyone can do it, and at times it seems that some cashiers are fifth formers on work experience.

> **Cashiers are there for one reason only: to serve customers who don't like using cash machines.**

They are there for one reason, and one reason only: to serve customers who don't like using cash machines. Yet anything not connected with physical cash (withdrawal, deposit, foreign currency for your holiday) will probably mean joining another queue to see a Personal Banker/Customer Services Advisor.

There are two occasions on which cashiers will break out of automated mode. When it's time for lunch, and when their till doesn't balance. Till discrepancies are the scourge of a cashier's life. Minor discrepancies of less than a pound are usually dealt with through a secret stash of coinage kept in a plastic coin bag under the watchful eye of the First Cashier. It is sometimes called the 'tea fund'. A 50p surplus in a till is simply resolved by taking the 50p and placing it in the 'tea fund', and everything is back to normal. A 20p shortfall sees the 'tea fund' debited accordingly. In some weeks very little might happen,

**66 Minor discrepancies of less than a pound are usually dealt with through the 'tea fund'. 99**

yet in others the 'tea fund' can outperform the stock market. (BCC a bit unlikely; ACC – After the Credit Crunch – not that difficult.)

Bluffers looking for some fun might mention the 'tea fund', particularly when an officious looking fellow in a pin-striped suit is standing behind a cashier. This is the bank inspector, who often pays a visit unannounced, and has to be kept away from the 'tea-fund' at all costs. Although keeping him away from the tea has an adverse effect.

## Personal bankers/customer service advisors

Bluffers must beware of falling for the seductive sales patter of a customer service advisor. These individuals are the holiday reps of banking and are there to help the bank sell products. They are salespeople. Forewarned is forearmed. Learn about the following scenarios considered to be 'sales opportunities' by the put-upon personal banker:

> **These individuals are the holiday reps of banking. They are salespeople.**

### Scenario 1

A naïve customer walks into a bank to notify them of a change of address. A successful customer service advisor will not let that person leave their desk until:

- Address details have been updated on the bank's computer.
- The customer has taken out home and buildings insurance for his/her new address.
- An appointment has been made with the mortgage specialist to see if the bank can beat the customer's existing mortgage deal with the bank's competitors.
- A credit card has been supplied to those without one, to help smooth the extra costs incurred when moving home, such as buying take-aways until the cooker is installed.

The bluffer will observe that what began as a simple relay of information has turned into a series of expensive and complicated transactions. And the bank may not even have got the new address right.

## Scenario 2

A customer complains of being charged £20 for going overdrawn by £150. The customer services advisor will offer to refund the charge if the customer applies for an authorised overdraft facility. While going through the application form, the advisor will spot:

- That the customer has two children. The aggrieved customer will then be offered an appointment with one of the bank's financial specialists to discuss life assurance, 'I'm sure as a responsible parent you wouldn't want your children to suffer should an unfortunate accident cause your untimely death.' (This should not be taken as a direct threat.)

> **"The advisor will offer a quote on a loan with their own friendly bank. 'Let's keep all your financial products together...'"**

- That a loan repayment is going to another bank. The advisor will offer a quote on a loan with their own friendly bank. 'Let's keep all your financial products together, and while we're at it let's add on the £150 by which you are overdrawn to bring you back into credit. In fact, let's make it £200 so you can eat tonight. Would you like any more money for anything else?'

The advisor, now fully into his or her stride, will then offer:

- Payment protection insurance for both the overdraft and the loan.
- A credit card to tide the customer over the few days at the end of the month when the overdraft at its limit and before the salary has gone in.

A smart bluffer would not be in this situation, but would tell friends who were that £20 is a small price to pay to avoid such a scenario.

## Scenario 3

A customer wants to update the bank with his or her new employment and work contact details. The customer services advisor will try to stay calm, while rubbing his hands together with glee beneath the table. Christmas has come early for the ambitious advisor.

- New jobs often mean higher salaries and higher salaries mean more disposable income, and the financial ability to repay bigger loans.
- Higher salaries also mean higher monthly outgoings and a higher standard of living. 'Better get the life insurance reviewed to ensure that your

surviving partner will still be able to afford this standard of living if you should suddenly die.'

- Higher salaries mean an ability to afford a greater contribution to your pension. 'Best make an appointment with a financial specialist to review pension arrangements.'

After updating the details, the unwary will leave with a new savings account and a standing order to transfer some money automatically on pay day, to all the products just purchased. You, on the other hand, will assure the advisor that your personal financial advisor has all these matters in hand, and leave.

## Telephone customer service operators

Modern technology means that call centres don't need to be in the same country as you are. You could be calling Bangor or Mumbai. Bluffers should keep contact with call centres to a minimum. Pressing the hash key may bypass all the automatic telephone menu options, but sometimes all it does is transfer you to a country where hash is grown.

## Mortgage specialists

Some serious bluffing is needed where mortgage specialists are concerned. Mortgages are regulated by the Financial Services Authority (FSA), which means that a mortgage specialist has to say a bit more than 'Your home may be a risk if you do not keep up the repayments on it,' although he or she will try to avoid spelling out the reality: 'If I don't offer you the best mortgage I could end up with a prison sentence.'

It was the mis-selling of endowment policy mortgages that led to this extra protection. Endowment policies relied on customers making a monthly payment towards the interest element of their mortgage, and then investing another monthly payment in the stock market. It was hoped that this stock market investment would grow and produce a large enough pot of money to repay the capital (the amount of money borrowed), by the end of the mortgage term. (You should note that those selling financial products like to talk about 'pots' and 'baskets'.)

**66 It's only fair that there is a mechanism in place for the bank to get it back if you should do something thoughtless – like die – before you've paid it off. 99**

Unfortunately, stock market prices can, as the small print has to divulge, go down as well as up, which is what happened to some investments – well, the down bit especially, and many customers discovered that they still owed thousands of pounds when their mortgage came to an end.

FSA regulations now mean that banks have to endeavour to offer the right mortgage for each customer's particular circumstances. To do this they need to know that customer inside out. But if a mortgage specialist gets up from his desk with a tape measure, to take your inside leg measurement, step away from the table, and make for the door. They don't need to know you that well.

The far-sighted bluffer should always take along the following information to any such meeting:

- Quotes for life assurance. In the bank's defence, it is lending you a lot of money, and it's only fair that there is a mechanism in place for the bank to get it back if you should do something thought-less – like die – before you've paid it off. Most mortgage providers insist upon life assurance. But life assurance doesn't have to be provided by the same bank – or any bank at all.

- Quotes for buildings insurance. Your property could be destroyed in a tornado if global warming continues apace, and then buildings insurance will enable you to rebuild the property on which the mortgage is held. The mortgage specialist will be very happy to sell you his bank's insurance. It might not be the cheapest, though.

- Mortgage quotes and offers from other banks. Not only does this suggest that you are a person that other financial institutions are willing to engage with, but it makes the mortgage specialist work harder to offer you a better deal.

The bluffer looking to re-mortgage should beware of special offers where banks offer you a case of champagne in lieu of cheaper monthly repayment than you currently have. Like bubbly, the offer is all fizz and no substance, and quite rapidly goes flat.

> 66 Beware of special offers where banks offer you a case of champagne in lieu of cheaper monthly repayment than you currently have. 99

Remember, too, that numbers can be manipulated. Extending the loan period reduces the monthly payment, for example. Borrow £60,000 over 25 years and your monthly repayments will be smaller than if you borrow the same amount over 15 years, but total repayments will cost more in the long run. Always compare like with like and ask the banker for a quote with exactly the same type of mortgage over the exact term. Bankers are (almost) human and they are as unlikely to have read the small print as the average customer (you, of course, are not the average customer), so to further accentuate the stratagem, ask him to explain the Terms and Conditions in detail. Or, better still, in layman's terms.

## Student officers

Student officers often look as if they've only just stopped being students themselves (because they often have). They have been there, done that, got the

T-shirt... and the debt, hence the need for a proper job. They like to feel they still have the ability to communicate with students and will therefore employ expressions they believe to be 'cool' but are in fact a few years out of date. Mimicry is the best form of flattery, so the student bluffer should adopt the same terminology. It may hurt, but it's worth it.

## Branch managers

Gone are the days when being a branch manager was a highly respected job entitling you to boss about other men in the Home Guard. These days, depending on the size of the branch, a branch manager may just be out of school (the ambitious type), or fighting off a midlife crisis (the promising-career-behind-him type).

> 66 Branch managers of smaller outlets have to be a jack-of-all-trades. Bluffers will quickly spot that this makes them a master of none. 99

Branch managers of smaller outlets often find themselves having to cover for members of their team at peak periods, at lunchtimes and outbreaks of staff sickness, which means they have to be a jack-of-all-trades. Bluffers will quickly spot that this makes them a master of none. A junior branch manager often has to ring a colleague up the road at the bigger branch for answers to questions they can't deal with.

This may also happen because the young manager has joined the bank on an 'accelerated training scheme'. This acceleration process sometimes means that they skip the basic stuff that school leavers have to contend with, such as the difference between a debit and a credit. A good ploy is to ask difficult questions, one at a time, and wait for them to put the phone down having found the answer to one question, before asking the next.

**❝You should not waste your time with big branch managers. Computers or regional offices make the real lending decisions.❞**

Small branch managers dream of becoming big branch managers. This is because big branch managers get an office with a door to keep out customers. However, gone are the days when they also had a secretary to bring in the mid-morning tea and a chocolate biscuit. They now have to type their own letters and get their own lunch. Although lunch, in the traditional go-out-and-sit-in-a-restaurant meaning of the word, is only for those whose branches meet their hourly sales targets.

You should not waste your time with big branch managers. They have no power. Computers or regional offices make the real lending decisions.

## Small business advisors

This is not a derogatory description of their stature. They are members of staff who don't want to get

40

involved in all that personal customer stuff and would much rather talk business – small business.

For many people, running their own business is a goal and a small business advisor can help them realise that dream. A sagacious bluffer should be wary, though, of taking advice about dreams from someone whose life appears somewhat prosaic. If they knew how to make dreams come true, they would not be stuck behind a desk flogging financial services, when they could be in control of their own destiny.

> **❝A sagacious bluffer should be wary of taking advice about dreams from someone whose life appears somewhat prosaic.❞**

Remember, too, that to succeed in business, you need to inspire confidence in yourself and your ideas. Be as creative as you possibly can with your business plan. Small business advisors love brightly coloured pictures and bar charts, and if you succeed in dazzling them, you're half way home.

## Business relationship managers

It follows that a small business advisor dreams of growing up to become a big business advisor, but the job title just doesn't cut the mustard in the corporate world. It's far too uncomplicated. Step forward the business relationship manager. Relationship is a strong word, with an established meaning. It means synchronising social arrangements, joining the same golf clubs, exchanging Christmas cards, and taking each other out to lunch from time to time. Any more than that and the relationship is on a different level, and not one with which we should concern ourselves here.

**❝ The aspiration of the business bluffer should be to upgrade from dealing with the small business advisor to the business relationship manager as soon as possible. ❞**

The aspiration of the business bluffer should be to upgrade him- or herself from dealing with the small business advisor to the business relationship manager as soon as possible. Learn golf, but play it badly so your new friend, the business relationship manager always wins. Be wary of nice lunches at the bank's expense. If you haven't paid for it in charges beforehand, you can be sure your charges will increase in the future to cover the cost.

## The private banking team

Most high street banks have a separate arm or sub-division, called the private banking team, that deals exclusively with 'high net worth customers'. High net worth individuals are what bluffers aspire to become, so you need to understand what the term means. Criteria vary, but if your annual salary, in thousands, is trebble that of your age (e.g., you are a

30-year-old earning £90,000), then you may be just the kind of customer they are looking for.

If you receive an invitation (and you have to be invited) to this private club, never turn it down. Service is superior. You don't queue up with the riff-raff, you ring your personal relationship manager on their mobile, at whatever time of day suits you. You will receive preferential treatment, better interest rates on savings and loans, and a whole host of products carefully tailored to your (presumed) needs. Here, you are not a number, but on first name terms. Such are the skills of the private banking team, they are more likely to remember your wedding anniversary than you are.

> **Such are the skills of the private banking team, they are more likely to remember your wedding anniversary than you are.**

Once in the club, the bluffer will rarely use cash, being too busy flashing designer credit and charge cards adorned with the words 'Private Banking' or 'Premier Banking'.

## Head office staff

Head office staff like to strategise (a popular word) and may be heard saying, when asked about their job, 'We do strategy'. Mostly, they attend meetings. To discuss things. Things like 'Implementation of the strategic agenda by organic growth and acquisition'. This is bank-speak for making more money by selling more products in the local market – financial products, not organic chard and free-range eggs – and by buying other financial businesses that may cost a lot but will, ceteris paribus make a lot more for the bank.

> **Mostly, head office staff attend meetings. To discuss things. Things like 'Implementation of the strategic agenda by organic growth and acquisition'.**

Ceteris paribus is a splendid expression, and one you could well use yourself. It means, of course, all things being equal, though they rarely are.

Of course, strategic financial decisions cannot be made lightly – or quickly. A meeting must take place to decide the terms of reference of any new project or venture. Then, there must be a meeting to decide who will be on the team to make the decision. A further meeting will decide who will do the research so that an informed decision may be made. Then there should be a meeting to decide whether or not external consultants need to be brought in (they will) to help inform the decision-making process. (This is extremely important as senior management can blame the external consultancy company and hence protect their own position, salary and bonuses if a strategy fails.)

Next there will be a meeting to agree the tender

process, to decide which external consultancy group should be employed, followed by a meeting to decide who should work with the external consultancy group. This is a role for internal middle management who are all delighted to be involved as they regard it as a step up the ladder of success. They, of course, will have a further series of meetings to outline the terms and framework of the project.

Once the project is established, meetings will multiply exponentially so head office staff can profile themselves to as many senior people as possible. (You need not concern yourself with what profiling themselves means.) And as a consensus needs to be reached among the various internal departments involved in the project – finance, marketing, IT – further meetings will be required. Reaching a consensus, though, is easier said than done as departments often operate 'in silos' and have their own agendas. 'In silos' is business consultant jargon with which the bluffer need not be concerned. Just be aware that it has nothing to do with storing grain.

> **Reaching a consensus is easier said than done as departments often operate 'in silos' and have their own agendas.**

If a project looks as if it is in trouble (which at this stage it is, as no work has been done because everyone has been busy attending meetings) those involved will remove themselves as far as possible so they are not associated with any perceived failure. Not that they need to move too fast as any failure will be the consultant's fault. Bluffers of an idle disposition will by now have identified a bank's head office as an ideal haven to find gainful employment.

# SOME TECHNICAL STUFF

## The mysteries of the clearing system

A cheque, according to the 1882 Bills of Exchange Act, is 'an unconditional order in writing, signed by the person giving it'. So, theoretically, the instruction to pay someone could be written on the back of a cow, although presenting it at a bank may prove difficult. Furthermore the cow itself may be of more value than the amount for which the cheque is written.

> **Theoretically, the instruction to pay someone could be written on the back of a cow, although presenting it at a bank may prove difficult.**

Though cheques are fast going out of fashion, they still have a role to play, so it is useful to have at your fingertips the inside information on a little understood scheme – the clearing system.

To the uninitiated, it seems that cheques are paid in at a bank and then fall into a no man's land where they battle to find their way back to the branch of the originating account. During the process, banks earn millions in interest, and customers lose access to money that is rightfully theirs.

Though this appears to be daylight robbery, bluffers can make it work to their benefit, by understanding the basics of the system.

Our old friend, the 1882 Bills of Exchange Act, required cheques to be physically returned to the branch of the bank where the account was held. In the heyday of cheques, this meant that the banks were constantly shifting piles of paper around the country.

**66** To the uninitiated, it seems that cheques are paid in at a bank and then fall into a no man's land where they battle to find their way back to the branch of the originating account. **99**

Let us imagine that a certain Mr Allworthy banks with a branch of HWest Bank, while Mr Goodenough has an account at Barcloyds Bank. If Mr Allworthy gives a cheque for £50 to Mr Goodenough the latter will pay it into his account at Barcloyds. The clearing system now has to transport Mr Allworthy's cheque back to the HWest Bank, a process that takes three days.

On day one the cheque is paid in at Mr Goodenough's Barcloyds bank where it is processed and his account is credited with the money. Overnight the cheque travels to the clearing centre

47

where it spends day two being sorted among millions of other cheques. It then travels back to Mr Allworthy's account at HWest Bank, where on day three, the money is taken out of that account. If attempting to explain this to a banking novice, you could employ paper and pencil during this discourse and sketch small buildings and stick people, as there is a danger that the other party may otherwise have nodded off.

> **A prudent bluffer would use the time difference to his or her advantage.**

A prudent bluffer will use the time difference to his or her advantage. Imagine the cheque being one for £50,000 instead of £50. Rather than transferring it to his current account on the day he writes the cheque, Mr Allworthy would keep this money in a savings account for as long as possible to earn the maximum interest on it. If he gives Mr Goodenough the cheque on Friday night the first opportunity he would have of banking it would be Monday. Even if Mr Goodenough's bank is open on Saturday, it won't be processed until Monday – see Business/Working days. So the earliest the cheque might arrive is Wednesday. Therefore, money need not be transferred from the prudent one's savings account until Tuesday, and extra interest can be earned on the money from Friday to Monday night.

Be aware that this wouldn't work if:

a) Mr Allworthy and Mr Goodenough have accounts at the same branch of the same bank. Should this be the case, the cheque is already at its account-holding branch and does not need to go through the clearing system. It will then appear on the recipient's statement and start earning interest on the day it is lodged, although it is usually the following day before the funds can be accessed – i.e., when the bank has been able to check that there are sufficient funds in the issuer's account to cover the cheque's value.

b) Mr Goodenough pays a charge to 'express' or 'specially present' the cheque.

The latter two services mean that the cheque avoids the clearing system and is sent directly to its account holding branch. Subject to the postal system working properly – hollow laughter at this point would not be inappropriate – the cheque could arrive at its destination branch the next day. Mr Goodenough should avoid using this service unless he needs the money in a hurry. Banks will be glad to charge for a service that merely entails sticking the cheque in an envelope and affixing a first class stamp.

> **66 Banks will be delighted to charge for a service that merely entails sticking the cheque in an envelope and affixing a first class stamp. 99**

The Deregulation (Bills of Exchange) Order 1996

removed the requirement for banks to physically return the cheque to its account holding branch. Despite this, the clearing times have not improved. Cynics may argue that it has something to do with the extra interest earned by banks on the money while it is in the clearing system. However, according to the Office of Fair Trading, the value earned from such cheque-related interest is negligible – a piece of information the educated bluffer could use for a little one-upmanship.

**66 When the banks needed to create an electronic system to transfer money between banks, they based it on the same three-day cycle used by the clearing system. Only a starry-eyed innocent would find this at all surprising. 99**

As bluffers know only too well, a good stratagem should be exploited to its fullest extent, so when, in the late 1960s, the banks needed to create an electronic system to transfer money between banks, they based it on the same three-day cycle used by the clearing system. Only a starry-eyed innocent would find this at all surprising.

The internet raised non-bluffer customer expectations, who demanded that if Google could search several trillion billion web sites in 0.02485 of a second, a bank should be able to transfer £50 by Standing Order in less than three days. Some 40 years after creating BACS, the new 'Faster

Payments' system was launched. This allows transfers made by telephone banking, internet banking and even standing orders to take place within hours. Of course, seasoned bluffers spotted the bluff a mile off and realised that only a handful of banks and building societies had joined the new scheme at its launch, making the service is about as useful as an Icelandic bank account during a credit crunch.

## Interest rates

Most people have little interest in banks at all until they need something that banks have lots of – money. And when a customer enters a bank looking for money, the bank becomes very interested indeed. It is wise, therefore, for the bluffer to take an interest in interest rates. This is because:

- Interest rates represent the real cost of borrowing money from a bank.
- Knowing the interest rates of a bank's competitors, puts you in a stronger position.
- Interest rates are the benefit of lending money back to the banks (in the form of savings).
- Interest rates rarely come in whole numbers, and decimal points make all the difference.
- Understanding interest rates will enhance your status with the uninitiated.

Banks know that consumers like a bargain. Decimals promote bargains, which is why interest rates are rarely quoted in whole numbers. To put it in shopping terms, if two identical items are on offer, one costing £10, the other costing £9.99, most consumers will go for the £9.99 item because it lurks just beneath the £10 barrier. This is a psychological trick that has been proved to work. An aspiring bluffer should learn to love decimals. All too often customers are lulled into thinking that the difference between 8.8% and 8.7% is negligible. Yet to a bank, that 0.1% difference is where the profit lies. Definitely not the difference between £9.99 and a tenner.

> **Banks know that consumers like a bargain. Decimals promote bargains, which is why interest rates are rarely quoted in whole numbers.**

Bankers have a term for these decimal percentages – they call them 'basis points'. These are usually written as 'bps' and are commonly referred to as 'BIPS'. One BIP, equates to 0.01%, an amount seemingly even more insignificant than 0.1%, but for someone with a mortgage of £250,000 over 30 years, this can equate to roughly £750 in interest repayments. So when the Bank of England announces a 25 basis point (or 0.25%) rate rise in the key lending rate, customers with variable rate loans can look forward to a similar rise in their loan rates and a commensurate rise in the monthly repayments. This is rather inconvenient – and why seasoned bluffers will consider fixed rates in a market-cycle of rising interest rates.

## Fixed or variable

Interest rates are available in two flavours – fixed and variable. Whether they are sweet or sour can only be measured over time. A loan fixed at 9% looks attractive when general interest rates rise to 15%, but if they then plummet to 4%, it can leave a sour taste. Until the time has passed, no one (not even the banks) can say whether the decision to go for a fixed rate was a good one or not. This is because a fixed interest rate, by defini-tion, doesn't change. It is about the only thing in banking that is certain (apart from bank charges).

> **66 Interest rates are available in two flavours – fixed and variable. Whether they are sweet or sour can only be measured over time. 99**

Variable rates of interest, on the other hand can, as the term suggests, move up or down. The longer the life of a loan, the greater the chances of movement up, down or indeed, in both directions. When interest rates move downwards, this is advantageous for the borrower, while any upward movement leaves the borrower a little more out of pocket. At this point any self-respecting bluffer begins looking for a better deal from another bank.

If asked for advice by a banking novitiate, employ the language of the finance world. Point out that 'In recent times rate trends have been upwards. If this continues, a borrower would be wise to avail himself of a fixed rate'. But be wary when bankers themselves use vague comments such as 'past trends' or 'no predictor of future movements', and ambiguous phrases like, 'if this contin-ues'. Use of such terminolo-gy is meant to suggest that bankers have provided robust advice whereas in fact they have done no such thing. They thereby avoid the threat of being told that they were wrong. Wise advice for the bluffer is, if you can't beat them, adopt their approach.

> **66 Use of such terminology is meant to suggest that bankers have provided robust advice whereas in fact they have done no such thing. 99**

As a general rule of thumb, it is an individual's disposition that is most important. Cautious or risk-averse borrowers should generally be pointed towards fixed rates, while the less cautious can be safely directed towards variable ones.

## Annual percentage rates (APRs)

APR is an acronym that is employed as if everyone knows and understands it. Few lay people do. Even bankers are loath to attempt an explanation, because not many of them do either. And even when they do, their explanations differ. Bluffers rightly baulk at such terminology becoming commonplace, because it represents the threat of being caught off guard, particularly if asked its meaning or, worse still, the difference between APR and the ordinary or headline rate. The following information, carefully digested, should stand you in good stead.

> **"Demanding to know the APR of a loan forces banks to put all their cards on the table and show their true hand."**

A loan with a headline interest rate of 5% may look good when compared with rival rates of 7%. However, it can be easy to overlook that there may be a £300 'arrangement fee' for taking the loan out in the first place. This is why all banks must, by law, quote the Annual Percentage Rate. The APR allows customers to compare directly the 'real' rates applicable between one loan and another.

The Annual Percentage Rate is the total cost of the loan over one year, expressed as a percentage and including all associated charges. It may be enough, when making this statement, to emphasise the words, 'annual' and 'total'. Demanding to know the APR of a loan forces banks to put all their cards on the table and show their true hand. It's an excellent opportunity to watch a discombobulated banker attempting to justify an interest rate less competitive than that of the bank next door, perhaps by suggesting that APR is 'a red herring that regulators seize upon to demonstrate how busy they are on a customer's behalf'.

> **66** All that really matters to potential borrowers is how much they will repay. **99**

All that really matters to potential borrowers is how much they will repay, whether it is cheaper than other options available, and if they can afford it. Financially focused bluffers should shop around, but only after the banker has finished squirming.

## Annual equivalent rate (AERs)

Bluffers with money to save (and thereby lend to a bank) should examine the Annual Equivalent Rate or A.E.R. This is because of what is called 'compound' interest. If you save £100 in an account that pays 5% interest, at the end of the year you will have £105 in your account. Keep the money there for another 12 months, and you will have – no, not £110, but £110.25 in your account. This is because during this second year, you've been earning 5% interest on the £5 interest that you earned last year, as well as your original £100. Getting the bank to pay interest on

> **66** Getting the bank to pay interest on the money they've already given you will make any bluffer quietly exultant. **99**

the money they've already given you will make any bluffer quietly exultant.

## Gross and net rates

As Benjamin Franklin once said: In life only two things are certain, death and taxes. You need not, at this stage, concern yourself with death, but you should be cognisant of the basics of taxation as it affects your bank balance. In very simple terms, HM Revenue & Customs takes a slice of the interest from every taxpayer, and a bigger slice from a higher rate taxpayer. Banks 'facilitate' this (bank speak for 'We'll make it easier for you and better for us') by taking the tax on interest at the standard rate and forwarding it to the taxman before you even see it in your account. Bluffers who aim to increase their wealth and become higher rate taxpayers should focus on the fact that with annual instead of quarterly interest taxes, they get the chance to earn extra interest on the taxable interest, before they have to relinquish it to the taxman.

> **❝The gross is the rate before the taxman has taken his share, the net is what you're left with afterwards. Or it could be what you fall through.❞**

Banks often quote both the 'gross' and 'net' rates. The gross rate is the rate before the taxman has taken his share, the net is what you're left with afterwards. Or it could be what you fall through.

## Business and working days

It is a fact universally acknowledged that if you are trading as a business, then you are working. A business day must therefore be a working day. Unless you are a bank.

**66 In banking a business day is not necessarily a working day. 99**

In the banking industry, a business day is not necessarily a working day. Some banks choose to classify some days as working days, and others as business days. Mondays to Fridays inclusive, are working days. Think of these as the days when the Banks Automated Credit System (BACS) is working. At weekends, despite it being automated, it takes a rest, does a bit of shopping, whips a duster around the house, plays with the kids and gets legless on a Saturday night if its football team loses again – which may explain the occasional system crash.

However, many banks have branches that are open on a Saturday. Saturday is not a working day because BACS has the weekend off, but for those banks that are open, Saturday is a trading day. So even if a cashier has banked your cheque for you on a Saturday, he wasn't actually working, merely carrying out the business of banking on a business day. Your transaction will therefore be held over to the next working day, which traditionally is a Monday, if it isn't a Bank Holiday, in which case it will be a Tuesday.

Bluffers can make use of this business/working day discrepancy. Those whose employers pay their salary by BACS into their account on a Monday can sometimes access these funds on the preceding Saturday. Technically, the salary doesn't reach the account until the Monday, but a cash point machine may allow a withdrawal against them. It is worth a try. But you better be quick. As it is clearly working in the customer's favour, the banks may even now be feverishly searching for a way round it.

## Bank holidays

A Bank Holiday is exactly what it says on the tin – a holiday for banks. The Bank of England used to close its doors on 33 occasions throughout the year to celebrate various saints' days and religious festivals. In 1834, however, this was cut to four, and remained so for several decades. This just wasn't cricket, particularly for Sir John Lubbock, a cricket-loving banker who believed staff should be able to enjoy the game. In Sir John's 1871 Bank Holiday Act several of the dates selected neatly coincided with dates when villages would settle scores with neighbouring communities with a bat and a ball and some wickets.

> **66 It was Sir John Lubbock, a cricket-loving banker who believed staff should be able to enjoy the game. 99**

So, the next time you're lying in bed until lunchtime on a Bank Holiday, raise your first cup of coffee to Sir John. It's because of him that you're not at work. Legitimately.

# MONEY MANAGEMENT TOOLS

It is said that a bad workman always blames his tools, but there is no point in blaming a bank for providing the wrong tools for the job. The consummate bluffer will know which ones are best suited and, more importantly, how to obtain and use them.

## Current accounts

The main tool in any bluffer's financial toolbox, current accounts are often free of charges as long as you are in credit. You will be offered a cheque book, which you might use occasionally, a cash point card, which you will use frequently, and a paying-in book that you may hardly ever touch.

> **To try to differentiate themselves, banks offer current accounts with bells and whistles. Some bells ring louder than others.**

The first step is to regulate your current account so that it contains only what is needed to meet regular outgoings and keep the rest of your cash in some form of savings account where it can work harder by earning good interest.

To try to differentiate themselves, banks offer current accounts with bells and whistles. Some bells ring louder than others. A current account may include:

- a small, interest-free overdraft facility
- a higher rate of interest on balances while in credit
- life assurance cover
- travel insurance
- preferential rates on loans
- car breakdown cover

The bluffer will, note, however, that with all these extra benefits 'Terms and conditions apply'. Terms and conditions always apply. Some banks charge a regular monthly fee. Others insist that a minimum amount is paid in every month. Decide which bell's chime is most appealing and choose accordingly.

## Cheques

Cheques are ailing, but they are not dead yet, and can still be a useful money management tool, not least for making payments to businesses and organisations that don't accept credit cards. They are also a useful prevarication tool for the financially embarrassed. Banks will 'bounce' cheques if funds are not available, but 'the funds must be caught up in the clearing system' excuse, and a polite request to the payee to re-lodge the cheque will give one another few days in which to identify a 25 to 1 winner at Newmarket.

## Banker's drafts

The only way for a bluffer to avoid receiving a bouncy cheque from another bluffer is to insist upon a banker's draft. These are only issued by a bank if there is money in the relevant account. They cannot be stopped unless the bank believes they may have been stolen. They are the closest financial instrument to cash and are often referred to as a 'cash equivalent'. However, you cannot use them in the pub. They are not that equivalent.

> **'The funds must be caught up in the clearing system' excuse will give one another few days.**

## Credit cards

Launched in 1966 by Barclaycard, credit cards ushered in an era of instant gratification and changed the word 'debt' (bad and nasty) into 'credit' (good and healthy). There is more than £50bn in debit balances outstanding on UK credit cards and the average person has as many credit cards as they do children

(2.4). Banks can instruct you to cut up your credit card if you get into severe debt but they are not allowed anywhere near your children.

Credit cards make life seem easy. You buy lots of nice things, book an exotic holiday, and when the bill arrives at the end of the month, all you have to pay is the minimum amount stipulated by the credit card company. The rest of the debt can be postponed – but at a price. In the same way that there is no such thing as a free lunch, there is no such thing, where banks are concerned, as a free loan.

This is where the banks make good money, and it is they who are the bluffers when they encourage customers to use credit cards as a way to borrow money, at interest rates sometimes three times as much as the rate charged for an unsecured loan. It's essential to bluff back, and a wily bluffer will realise that paying credit card bills in full each month is the way forward.

> **In the same way that there is no such thing as a free lunch, there is no such thing, where banks are concerned, as a free loan.**

Credit cards are not just useful tools, they avoid the need to carry large amounts of cash about with you. If the card is lost or stolen it can be stopped to prevent fraudulent use, and, under the Consumer Credit Act of 1974 customers purchasing goods over £100 in value on a credit card can claim the money back from the card issuer if the supplier fails to deliver the goods or goes bust.

Beguiling offers can be manipulated. Zero percent interest rate on balance transfers encourages people to 'transfer the balance' (move their debt) from one card to another, while paying no interest on that transferred debt for a fixed period. Play the banks at their own game and use a credit card to your advantage, not theirs.

The best credit cards for bluffers who wish to remain free of debt are the cash-back ones. Here the bank or credit card company will give you a rebate as a percentage of your total spending on the card. A rebate of 0.5% doesn't sound much, but spend £15,000 on a credit card over 12 months, and a 0.5% refund of £75 is very welcome.

**❝A careful bluffer will switch to cash-back cards. Instead of paying the banks for the privilege of using their product, they pay you. ❞**

A careful bluffer will not spend money he or she doesn't have on a credit card, but will switch existing spending to their cash-back cards. Instead of paying the banks for the privilege of using their product, they pay you. This is a most satisfactory manoeuvre.

## Debit cards

There are more debit cards in the UK than people. They are extremely useful tools, especially as most do not incur the fee that is often charged for online transactions.

Originally marketed as the electronic cheque, the debit card made writing cheques obsolete. Fearing that consumers couldn't cope with the concept of instant payments, a delay was built in so that debit card transactions were processed like cheques, debiting accounts a few days after the actual transaction. Bluffers will be aware of this, but should have no objection to banks making money through the clearing system on money that hasn't yet been debited from their accounts.

> **Fearing that consumers couldn't cope with the concept of instant payments, a delay was built in so that debit card transactions were processed like cheques.**

## Personal identification numbers (PINs)

PINs are not unique. The numbers 0 to 9 are used to create a 4-digit code, which means that the number of variations is limited. In the UK, several thousand will have the same PIN as you, although it is to be hoped that they won't have your card as well. Such is the human brain's incapacity to remember 4-digit numbers that banks permit cardholders to generate their own, one that they find more memorable. To prevent a thief from accessing all your cash, it is a wise bluffer who uses a different PIN for each card.

Those thinking that to use the year of their birth as their 'secret' PIN is a cunning ruse would do well to consider that this is the 'system' most used by cardholders – and therefore the most likely code to be cracked. It's a number to be avoided.

## Automated teller machines (ATMs)

Usage of ATMs is at its highest on weekend evenings. If you incorrectly enter your personal identification number several times in a row (usually three), the ATM will gobble it up. The idea is to prevent an unauthorised user from working out your PIN by pure guesswork and hence accessing available funds. Nine times out of ten, however, it is you, the valid cardholder, who has made several valiant but unsuccessful attempts to remember your own code. Strangely enough, this loss of memory also reaches its peak on weekend evenings, particularly just after the pubs have closed.

**66 The ATM facility is one of the great breakthroughs in banking – something that is actually a convenience. 99**

## Standing orders

Standing Orders take the nuisance out of making regular payments. Standing orders between accounts at the same bank usually take place on the same day. Payments to accounts at other banks may take up to three days by those institutions who've elected not to join the Faster Payments system, during which time they can increase their profits further. They know it pays dividends.

## Direct debits

These are another clever banking product under the guise of helping customers to pay 'variable' bills.

Once set up, Direct Debits can give anyone authority to take money from an account automatically by 'raising' a direct debit on that account. This is when life becomes interesting. The provider can take any

> **66 It's easier to get a loan if you already have the money to pay it back, which is ironic since this is when you least need it. 99**

amount, on any day – well, any business day – from your account. So check your bank statements. Often.

# BORROWING

It's easier to get a loan if you already have the money to pay it back, which is ironic since this is when you least need it. If you've never borrowed any money before, you are a higher risk because you don't have a track record of paying it back. Consider this a contemporary Catch-22 situation.

Modern technology enables banks to pass the decision-making process for the vast majority of their loans to their computers. Bank staff much prefer this because the 'computer says no' principle means that they don't bear the responsibility for your disappointment. It allows them to convey the impression that if it were up to them, instead of a heartless machine, they would be pleased to oblige.

**❝Your credit score is not an inherent thing, like a cholesterol rating.❞**

Banks use a credit scoring system, whereby points are awarded for the answers you give on an application form. It is this information that is fed into their computers. Your credit score is not an inherent thing, like a cholesterol rating. It is based upon the information that you give, and any other information available to the computer.

Bluffing your way to a loan means giving the right information. While ensuring that the information is accurate, you can still influence it in a positive way:

- How much do you need?
  You will have costed this carefully beforehand. It's going to cost you in interest, so the less you borrow, the less of a risk you are, the less you have to pay back and the less it will cost overall. Less is more.

- What do you need the money for?
  Remember that bankers like conformity, so sticking to the usual options – weddings, cars, holidays and kitchen extensions – tend to be the safest bet.

- How long do you need to pay it back?
  The longer you borrow the money for, the more interest you will pay even though the monthly repayments are lower. Prudent bluffers will borrow over shorter periods.

- What are your personal circumstances?
  A single person living in furnished, rented accommodation may be seen as a higher risk because all they have to do is pack a suitcase to do a moonlight flit. In the bank's view a married person in a stable job with a mortgaged house and two kids at school, would find it much more difficult to disappear. Chances are, they'd cancel the papers and tell someone where they were going anyway. There is little you can do to put a good gloss on this area of information, however, short of getting married and taking out a mortgage. And if you could afford to do that you probably wouldn't need the loan in the first place.

- What's your income?
  This, of course, is designed to see whether you can afford the monthly repayment. Bluffers will

realise that it is advantageous, and not dishon-
est, to include all forms of income, e.g., child
benefit and a spouse's income, along with their
salary

• What are your outgoings?
This means everything that leaks out of your
account. Mortgage, utilities, mobile phone, food,
gym membership. Not much you can do (as an
honest bluffer) to make this sound better than it
is. But you could cut out the gym membership.
You probably don't use it anyway.

• What's left?
The bank's highly sophisticated computer system
will take away your total monthly outgoing figure from your total monthly income figure to see
what's left. If you spend more than you earn, you
can't afford to pay back a loan and the sophisticated system will recommend that you acquire a
better-paid job. If you earn more than you spend,
then with careful husbandry, you should be asking for a savings account, not a loan.

## Overdrafts

There are two types of overdraft – authorised and
unauthorised. Authorised overdrafts are what the
bluffer should go for. They are considerably cheaper

than unauthorised ones because you've taken the time to beg for the bank's permission to go over-drawn, even grovelling a bit, if necessary. Banks like this. It's a power thing.

On the other hand, banks also like unauthorised overdrafts, because they can demonstrate their authority through charges – higher fees and higher interest rates. It is worth a bit of grovelling to avoid this.

## Unsecured loans

This is one of the most common types of loans offered – so common that insurance companies, motoring organisations and high street stores as well as banks all vie to lend you money. The bluffer will spot that the word 'unsecured' is the key to their popularity. If you take one out, your home is not at risk.

Bankers get excited over unsecured loans because of the extra insurance they can sell you. This is often referred to as

> **Bankers get excited over unsecured loans because of the extra insurance they can sell you.**

'payment protection' and is highly profitable – for the banking industry. The insurance offers to pay off the loan in full, or continue making monthly pay-ments, usually for 12 months, should you be made redundant or are unable to work due to ill health.

Payment protection will even pay off the loan if you die. You wouldn't care at that stage but your nearest and dearest would probably be relieved.

For some bluffers this is a sensible option (taking out insurance, not dying). For the banks, it is a security net, and a gold mine. Imagine that the payment protection on a £5,000 loan costs £250. The £250 charge is added to your loan, which means that you are borrowing £5,250. Not only are you paying extra on your loan for the insurance, but the bank is now charging you interest on the insurance protection.

> **Payment protection will even pay off the loan if you die. For some bluffers this is a sensible option. For the banks, it is a security net, and a gold mine.**

If you decide to take out the insurance, write out a cheque for the total insurance cost and avoid paying this extra charge. Alternatively, shop around for insurance from another bank. A bluffer who says, 'I've already arranged the insurance elsewhere,' will have the upper hand. Few borrowers show this acumen, and the banker will (metaphorically) doff his cap to you and move on.

Be on your guard, too, against banks that quote the monthly loan repayments figures inclusive of insurance. The unwary who take up such offers will have bought two products at the same time. Clearly, this is not the kind of 'two for one' offer a bluffer wants.

If you were to borrow money from a friend and, having received a windfall from the lottery or the demise of Aunt Ada, wanted to pay it back rapidly, the friend would surely be delighted. But if you obtain a fixed bank loan and wish to pay it back early the bank may apply an 'early redemption' penalty where the term is deemed to have been 'broken' – in other words, they've lost the opportunity to charge you interest.

## Mortgages

I want a mortgage,' is a statement many bankers hear. Nothing could be further from the truth. Nobody wants a mortgage. For the aspiring home-owner a mortgage is a loan to buy a house. It is also the start of a relationship that may last longer than most marriages. For a bank, it is a licence to print money for anything up to 40 years.

> **A mortgage is also the start of a relationship that may last longer than most marriages.**

Bluffers who are prepared to make this commitment to their banker (for richer, for poorer, but usually poorer) should spend some time thinking about the kind of relationship they wish to embark upon.

**Variable rate** This kind of relationship has its ups and downs. If the Bank of England raises interest rates, then your mortgage interest rate will rise, your monthly payment will increase, and you'll feel poorer. If the Bank of England reduces interest rates, your mortgage rate will fall and you will feel a little wealthier at the end of the month. But not much.

**Fixed rate** This is the steady, dependable kind of relationship. Or, at least, it starts out that way. Fixed rate mortgages are not subject to sudden fluctuations. If the Bank of England raises interest rates, the monthly payments of those with variable rate mortgages go up, but yours stay the same. This is one of the rare occasions when you can feel financially smug. However, in the mortgage market, as in life, there is no such thing as a perfect relationship. If interest rates fall, your payments won't. The bank will have a smile on its corporate face. Fixed rate mortgages, therefore, tend to be short-lived affairs of between one and five years. Think of them as romantic interludes.

> **❝In the mortgage market, as in life, there is no such thing as a perfect relationship. If interest rates fall, your payments won't.❞**

**Capped rate** This is the kind of relationship that offers the best of both worlds. The interest rate is fixed so that it can't increase above a specified amount, but it is also variable, so if interest rates fall below this capped rate, your mortgage repayment will drop too. In practice, and for obvious reasons, banks usually only offer this advantageous deal for a short period, after which you have to start renegotiating. Cap in hand, of course.

## SAVINGS

Banks need savers so they can lend their money to borrowers. The way in which you chose to save depends whether you are one of life's gamblers, or not.

### Stocks and shares

Shares in successful banks are an attractive option. Whilst beauty may be in the eye of the beholder, a credit crunch tends to produce better than 20/20 vision and their attractiveness can drop through the floor just like their share price. Such price variations mean that a banker won't offer any real clarity about potential future performance, particularly their own. Bankers can do ambiguity just as well as bluffers. In betting parlance, a score–draw between bluffer and banker.

> **Price variations mean that a banker won't offer any real clarity about potential future performance, particularly their own.**

Amateur bluffers who are more risk-averse need

to look away from stocks and shares, and consider safer options. 'Risk-averse', incidentally, is part of banking jargon, and may be used with impunity.

## Best buy tables

Nothing to do with discount-price furniture, but lists showing which banks offer the best rates for which products. The wise bluffer will spot two trends:

1 No single bank dominates the top spot in every table for every product, and cunning bluffers will hedge their bets.

2 A bank is rarely a 'best buy' for a long period. Many banks will tempt you with a top of the league table interest rate, then drop it to a less competitive level as soon as you take your eye off the ball. Bluffers will stay vigilant and transfer to those in the higher rate divisions.

> **Many banks will tempt you with a top of the league table interest rate, then drop it to a less competitive level as soon as you take your eye off the ball.**

The risk-averse will place their savings in safer deposit-type 'products' that offer low rates of return. Here capital is guaranteed but, with the rates usually being below the rate of inflation, over time the purchasing power of the savings will diminish, a situation no self-respecting bluffer would countenance.

## Instant access accounts

Interest rates on some of these accounts may be lower than the current rate of inflation. If, therefore, you prudently decide to defer for 12 months the purchase of a coveted digital radio that costs £100 and deposit that money in an instant access account offering 2% interest, you will have £102 by the end of the year. But if inflation is running at 3% a year the radio will cost £103. So

> **Banks like to think of higher rates for notice accounts as rewarding your loyalty for letting them hold on to your money for longer. Bluffers view it as ransom money.**

you will be £1 out of pocket and will have denied yourself 12 months' pleasure with your new digital toy. Canny bluffers will only save if the rate of interest is higher than the rate of inflation. If it isn't, buy the radio and get tuned in.

## Notice accounts

The most noticeable thing about notice accounts are higher rates of interest, in return for which you have to give notice – usually 30, 60 or 90 days – that you want to withdraw your money. Banks like to think of this as rewarding your loyalty for letting them hold on to your money for longer. Bluffers view it as ransom money. Unsurprisingly, the higher the ransom money paid by the banks, the longer they hold it hostage.

## Individual savings accounts (ISAs)

Amazingly, accounts that you don't have to declare on your tax return. Savvy bluffers know there are two types: cash and stocks and shares. The cash ISA allows you to save without paying tax on the interest earned, but you can't squirrel away more than the annual limit, which the Chancellor of the Exchequer reviews from time to time. The stocks and shares ISA is also variable and limited.

> **Bluffers should be wary of impressively high rates: it could imply what one's advisor would term 'an element of risk'.**

Alternatively, you could have one large stocks and shares ISA. This has the same overall limit as the two smaller ones added together, but can only be used for stocks and shares. Do not be bamboozled by this into thinking your money would be better off in a piggy bank. ISAs mean you pay less tax, ergo, bluffers should have ISAs.

## Bonds

Bonds earn the highest interest rate of all, but you need to bid farewell to your money for years. Bluffers should be wary of impressively high rates: it could imply what a bank advisor would term 'an element of risk'. Ideally, the only risk you should be looking at is whether the interest rate offered is enough to beat the inflation rate during the period that your money is off enjoying itself elsewhere.

# THE WIDER BANKING WORLD

Most bluffing opportunities arise in dealings with the
high street banks. However, as banking is a global
industry, to maximise opportunities the bluffer should
be able to take an international view.

## The banking code of practice

Banks can volunteer to practice this, but they don't
have to if they don't want to. Bluffers should only use
those who do because practice makes perfect.

## Merchant banks

Merchant bankers are not usually interested in individuals but in huge corporations that finance companies with grand plans. Names such as Rothschild and
Goldman Sachs are synonymous with the merchant
banking industry. So was Barings whose $1.3 billion
loss was chicken feed when compared to the $700
billion or so that the American taxpayer had to under-
pin the banks by during the credit crunch. It doesn't
take a particularly perceptive bluffer long to realise
that betting on the sub-prime market being able to
repay its debts was, in hindsight, the biggest banking
bluff of all time. Cockney rhyming slang bluffers living
in the East end of London have always known the true
meaning of the phrase 'merchant banker'.

## Financial services compensation scheme

The Financial Services Compensation Scheme operates the Deposit Protection Scheme, which means that if a bank collapses, the scheme will cover the first £50,000 of an investor's savings. As the scheme covers £50,000 per bank, bluffers with more to invest should bear in mind adages about eggs and baskets.

## Central banks

The role of the central banks is a patriarchal one – to maintain economic calm by controlling interest rates and monitoring exchange rates.

**" Aside from a pint of bitter, cash is the most liquid asset you can have. "**

To ensure this happens, central banks insist that high street banks keep a percentage of their assets in liquid form to counteract a 'run' on banks as witnessed with Northern Rock. Suffice it to say that the more 'liquid' an asset, the easier it is to turn into cash. Aside from a pint of bitter, cash is the most liquid asset you can have – which is why it flows out of your pocket so easily.

## Bank for International Settlements

The BIS is the godfather of all banks. Its head office is located in one of the most famously secretive of banking domains, Switzerland. Among other functions, it acts as a meeting place for central bankers to

encourage international monetary and financial coop-
eration. This means that thousands of senior executives and officials from central banks have to jet off to
Basel for in-depth discussions
and a good lunch.

> **The principles of Basel 1 and Basel 2 are so complicated that whole departments are dedicated to their deciphering and implementation.**

The BIS has negotiated two
key agreements, imaginatively
named Basel 1 and Basel 2, the
principles of which must be
adopted by all banks. These principles are so complicated that
whole departments are dedicated to their deciphering
and implementation, and the bluffer should not
dream of trying to understand them. Too much
knowledge is highly undesirable. If you are ever
accosted by a 'Basel' advocate, advise him or her that
you are currently working on the new agreement,
Basel 7. This serves to identify you as a person in the
know, while wrong-footing your interlocutor who was
not aware of the existence of Basel 3 to 6. Bluffing
doesn't get much more satisfying than this.


## International rating agencies

All banks desire to be 'rated' as highly as possible, in
the same way a bluffer expects to obtain a high credit
score. Three companies are recognised worldwide in
providing such ratings – Standard & Poors, Moodys,

and Fitch Rating. These ratings range from AAA down to D (in league table terms the equivalent of Chelsea or Man United at the one end and Dagenham & Redbridge at the other).

Triple A organisations are perceived as so financially sound, they almost have a licence to print money. It is with these 'institutions' (never use the word 'bank' in conversations at this level) that bluffers should aim to deal. It will enhance your standing if you bandy about the term Triple A. Do so with confidence and don't get confused. Remember that AAA is the pinnacle, whereas AA, of course, refers either to a motoring organisation or Alcoholics Anonymous.

> 66 It is with these 'institutions' (never use the word 'bank' in conversations at this level) that bluffers should aim to deal. 99

## The World Bank

The World Bank is not a traditional bank. It was set up in 1944 to help rebuild countries devastated by the Second World War. Today its role is to tackle worldwide poverty, and offer low interest loans to the poorest countries. This is, of course, an altruistic and Good Thing. But remember, it is only when the world's poor have become rich, that the world's banks can make even bigger profits. In the long run, banks, like bookies, rarely lose. You can bank on it.

# GLOSSARY

**Bad debts**  Unpaid credit facilities (loans, etc). Bad for the bank, bad for shareholders and extremely bad for the customer in the long run.

**Banking instruments**  Technically, banks don't have products – they have instruments. Not the type you might find in the Royal Philharmonic, but of the cheque, draft and deposit variety. The trick is to learn how to orchestrate them.

**Bank opening times**  Slightly shorter than the average working day, which means that most people have to go to the bank in the lunch hour, when half the bank's employees are having their own lunch.

**Credit crunch**  Credit as in borrowing ability and crunch as in painful constriction. A not-so-short sharp shock to the ability of banks around the world to borrow from each other, in turn making it more difficult and more expensive for the ordinary customer to obtain a loan.

**Dormant accounts**  Accounts in which no transactions have taken place for a long time. Often forgotten by the customers for several decades, they usually contain very little money.

**Duty of confidentiality**  Banks will only tell you what they think you should know.

**EMU**  European Monetary Union. The framework for the Euro established by the Maastricht Treaties of 1992. Like the Australian bird of the same name it has great difficulty staying airborne.

**European Central Bank**  Modelled loosely on Germany's Bundesbank, the ECB is responsible for monetary policy in the EMU.

**Free banking**  Beware, it's usually nothing of the sort. Should be seen as 'free' in the sense that the National Health Service, is free at the point of delivery, but you pay for it on a regular basis.

**Impairment losses**  See Bad Debts.

**Internet banks**  The ones that have moved 'from bricks to clicks'.

**Investment adviser**  A wolf in wolf's clothing.

**L.I.B.O.R.** (London Inter Bank Ordinary Rate)  The rate of interest banks charge each other when lending money between themselves on the wholesale market. Usually a LIttle BORing except during a credit crunch when high rates suggest that the banks don't trust one another – so neither should bluffers.

**Offshore accounts**  An absolute misnomer, as the accounts are never held at sea but rather in a bank in some exotic sounding location, usually for the purpose of avoiding tax.

**Phishing**  Bogus e-mails which try to trick the recipients into revealing their password or PIN.

**Redemption**  When paying off a mortgage the banker considers the mortgage as 'redeemed' while the customer finds real redemption – liberation.

**Relationship Manager (RM)**  Bank employee whose job is to ensure you maintain your relationship with his/her bank, rather than starting a new one with another bank.

**Repayment capacity**  The concept of the borrower's ability to repay a loan. Usually based upon current earnings and the likelihood that the borrower will remain earning at least an equivalent salary for the duration of the loan (thus precluding actors and many of the self-employed) and will not decide to move to Tibet to find him- or herself.

**Retail banking**  General day-to-day banking services (accounts, credit cards and loans). Not to be confused with retail therapy as it has little therapeutic quality. Tends also to contain a non-return, non-refund policy.

**Saving**  Best left to goalkeepers.

**Secure loan**  A loan that is 'collateralised' against something of value. Effectively, a posh form of pawn broking.

**Terms and conditions**  Referred to by those in the know as 'Ts & Cs', these cover the small print of every product, service and transaction the customer conducts with the bank. It's the gentlemanly way of not having to call in the heavies to ensure that agreements are honoured.

**Transaction analysis**  Nothing to do with banking at all despite the transaction word. Rather it's the 'parent/adult/child' theory founded by Eric Berne. It has wide applications in clinical, therapeutic, organisational and personal development, encompassing communications, management, personality, relationships and behaviour. (Actually, quite a lot to do with banking, then).

**Unsecure loan**  A bigger risk for banks because you don't have to hand over any assets to get your hands on the money. If you default, the bank may sue you, but at least it can't evict you. It will, however, ensure that the credit reference agencies know all about you, so no-one else will lend you any money no matter how smart a suit you are wearing.

# THE AUTHORS

A pragmatic optimist, sports addict and novice saxophone player, **Robert Cooper** has busied himself in the financial world for nigh on a quarter of a century. Because he knows the wrinkles (both his own and the bank's), others expect him to be wealthy as well as wise. Not a bit of it. His bank accounts are as chaotic as everyone else's.

As a bank employee, he was automatically in receipt of bank shares. He realises being a customer, shareholder sand employee simultaneously could be said to be a conflict of interest which he ought to point out to the banking world. But won't.

As a Personal Banker, **Simon Whaley** spent December flogging credit cards to customers to give them the best Christmas ever, and January trying to convert all those huge credit card bills into unsecured loans (with payment protection and any other insurance he could think of.) He worked in several branches, which enabled him to serve celebrities such as Hayley Mills, Frank Carson and the bloke that played the barman in *Only Fools and Horses*.

Now a full-time writer, he spends his spare time juggling the few pounds he has in his bank accounts (using insider knowledge gained during his banking career) to try and keep his platinum credit card, without actually having a platinum income to match it.

### Negotiation

You may need to explain why your detailed plans were jettisoned. Put this down to a 'battleground decision' (a versatile phrase to which you should become wedded) or 'creative genius'. If at all possible, try not to admit to 'winging it'.

### Consultancy

Always be hard to get. A blank diary must be made to seem full. Bogus meetings must be cancelled or postponed. You must always appear to have had to tear yourself away from urgent and important matters to attend to your client's needs.

### Bond

Foodwise, Bond may well like the simple stuff but if possible he would like it to be of the highest quality – not just not just any eggs, but deep brown eggs with a rich yellow yolk laid by French hens of the Maran breed; not just smoked salmon, but Scottish smoked salmon, cured in the Highlands. Connery would have approved.

### Management

The acid test of the true manager under pressure is that he or she is the only one not immediately doing something. The real manager is thinking before acting. Even if it's only a bluff.

### Accountancy

The high point of accountancy is double-entry book-keeping, whose unique merit is that the debits are balanced by credits in other accounts; not the same ones, or the limited intellectual challenge would have vanished altogether.

### Golf

On the green manoeuvres are minimal. You are, of course, allowed to pick up the ball to clean it and a few inches may be gained this way. Always put the marker down in front of the ball but replace the ball in front of the marker. Even most professionals do this as the action is not usually closely watched.

## Quantum Universe:
"Very much enjoyed. It opens a window onto the astounding things that are happening in the world."
Reader from Hampshire

## Archaeology:
"Hilarious truths that archaeologists have tried hard to keep hidden from the public for many years. Having been involved myself, it made me howl with recognition."
Reader from Sheffield, UK

## Marketing:
"Any marketing person who has not read this book has almost certainly wasted their time and money reading all the others. It's funny, witty, and true.
Reader from London

## Public Speaking:
"Good tips for those who have do presentations every once in a while. How to act if everything fails including electricity, etc. And of course very enjoyable to read."
Reader from The Netherlands

## Music:
"Everything you need to know about the major composers with all the right things to say. Extremely witty and well written."
Reader from Los Angeles

# the Bluffer's® Guides

## Oval Books

*This Bluffer's® Guide is available as a downloadable audiobook: **www.audible.co.uk/bluffers**

We like to hear from our readers.
Please send us your views on our books
and we will publish them as appropriate on
our web site: ovalbooks.com.

Oval Books also publish the best-selling
Xenophobe's Guide® series –
see www.ovalbooks.com

Both series can be bought via Amazon or directly
from us, Oval Books through our web site
www.ovalbooks.com or by contacting us.

Oval Books charges the full cover price
for its books (because they're worth it) and
£2.00 for postage and packing on the first
book. Buy a second book or more and postage
and packing will be entirely FREE.

To order by post please fill out the accompanying
order form and send to:
Oval Books
5 St John's Buildings
Canterbury Crescent
London SW9 7QH

cheques should be made payable to: Oval Books

or phone us on +44 (0)20 7733 8585
or visit our web site at: www.ovalbooks.com

Payment may be made by Visa or Mastercard and orders are
dispatched as soon as the card details and mailing address are
received. If the mailing address is not the same as the card holder's
address it is necessary to give both.

Oval Books